MANGA MAGIC

DRAWING MANGA
BOYS

ANNA SOUTHGATE AND KEITH SPARROW

rosen publishing's
rosen central®

NEW YORK

This edition published in 2012 by:

The Rosen Publishing Group, Inc.
29 East 21st Street
New York, NY 10010

Additional end matter copyright © 2012 by The Rosen Publishing Group, Inc.

Library of Congress Cataloging-in-Publication Data

Southgate, Anna.
Drawing manga boys / Anna Southgate, Keith Sparrow.
    p. cm.—(Manga magic)
Includes bibliographical references and index.
ISBN 978-1-4488-4799-0 (library binding)
ISBN 978-1-4488-4803-4 (pbk.)
ISBN 978-1-4488-4807-2 (6-pack)
1. Comic books, strips, etc.—Japan—Technique—Juvenile literature. 2. Drawing—Technique—Juvenile literature. 3. Boys in art—Juvenile literature. I. Sparrow, Keith. II. Title.
NC1764.5.J3S675 2011
741.5'1—dc22

                                                                    2011010862

Manufactured in the United States of America

CPSIA Compliance Information: Batch #S11YA: For further information, contact Rosen Publishing, New York, New York, at 1-800-237-9932.

All other content copyright © 2007 Axis Publishing Limited, London.

CONTENTS

INTRODUCTION

Samurais, space cowboys, and school kids are just a few of the different types of boys that appear in manga books. Manga (pronounced mahn-gah) comes from Japan. It's an art style in comics and graphic novels known for it's sharp features and expressive figures. Stylistically, manga boys are usually slim in build, but they can be powerhouses with big muscles, or little elf-like sprites. Manga boys can even have feminine features, too. Nothing is outside the realm of possibilities! It just depends on your ability to commit your ideas to paper with pencil and ink. This guide will take you through the fun learning process of creating and crafting your manga boys step-by-step.

Much of the character's personality comes through in his appearance. Is he neat and well groomed or does he have a wild mane of bright-red hair? Is he a ninja who wears dark colors to help sneak around or a regal prince who dons his land's colors proudly? They say that eyes are the windows to the soul and that's extremely true of manga characters. Manga characters characteristically have large, emotive eyes. Perhaps your monster hunter character has a fire in his eyes to match his bad temper? With these limitless possibilities, the skills and methods you acquire using this book will make drawing a school-aged, futuristic, time-traveling, space ace a piece of cake!

You do not need to spend a fortune to get started in drawing and coloring good manga art. You do, however, need to choose your materials with some care to get the best results from your work. Start with a few basics and add to your kit as your style develops and you figure out what you like working with.

Artists have their preferences when it comes to equipment, but regardless of personal favorites, you will need a basic set of materials that will enable you to sketch, ink, and color your manga art. The items discussed here are only a guide—don't be afraid to experiment to find out what works best for you.

PAPERS

You will need two types of paper—one for creating sketches, the other for producing finished color artwork.

For quickly jotting down ideas, almost any piece of scrap paper will do. For more developed sketching, though, use tracing paper. Tracing paper provides a smooth surface, helping you to sketch freely. It is also forgiving—any mistakes can easily be erased several times over. Typically, tracing paper comes in pads. Choose a pad that is around 24 pounds (90 grams per square meter) in weight for best results—lighter tracing papers may buckle and heavier ones are not suitable for sketching.

Once you have finished sketching out ideas, you will need to transfer them to the paper you want to produce your finished colored art on. To do this, you will have to trace over your pencil sketch, so the paper you choose cannot be too opaque or "heavy"—otherwise you will not be able to see the sketch underneath. Choose a paper around 16 lb (60 gsm) for this.

Graphite pencils are ideal for getting your ideas down on paper and producing your initial drawing. The pencil drawing is probably the most important stage in creating your artwork. Choose an HB and a 2B to start with.

The type of paper you use is also important. If you are going to color using marker pens, use "marker" or "layout" paper. Both of these types are very good at holding the ink found in markers. Other papers of the same weight can cause the marker ink to "bleed," that is, the ink soaks beyond the inked lines of your drawing and produces fuzzy edges. This does not look good.

You may wish to color your art using other materials, such as colored pencils or watercolors. "Drawing" paper is good for graphite pencil and inked-only art (such as

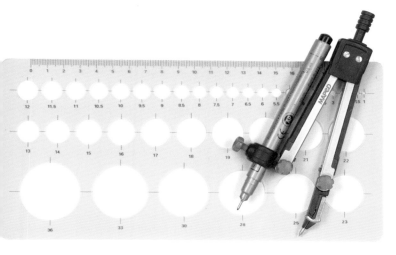

Working freehand allows great freedom of expression and is ideal when you are working out a sketch, but you will find times when precision is necessary.

Use compasses or a circle guide for circles and ellipses to keep your work sharp. Choose compasses that can be adjusted to hold both pencils and pens.

that found in the majority of manga comic books), while heavyweight watercolor papers hold wet paint and colored inks and come in a variety of surface textures.

Again, don't be afraid to experiment: you can buy many types of papers in single sheets while you find the ones that suit your artwork best.

PENCILS

The next step is to choose some pencils for your sketches. Pencil sketching is probably the most important stage, and always comes first when producing manga art (you cannot skip ahead to the inking stage), so make sure you choose pencils that feel good in your hand and allow you to express your ideas freely.

Pencils are manufactured in a range of hard and soft leads. Hard leads are designated by the letter H and soft leads by the letter B. Both come in six levels—6H is the hardest lead and 6B is the softest. In the middle is HB, a halfway mark between the two ranges. Generally, an HB and a 2B lead will serve most sketching purposes, with the softer lead being especially useful for loose, "idea" sketches, and the harder lead for more final lines.

Alternatively, you can opt for mechanical pencils. Also called self-propelling pencils, these come in a variety of lead grades and widths, and never lose their points, making sharpening traditional wood-cased pencils a thing of the past. Whether you use one is entirely up to you—it is possible to get excellent results whichever model you choose.

SHARPENERS AND ERASERS

If you use wooden pencils, you will need to get a quality sharpener; this is a small but essential piece of equipment. Electric sharpeners work very well and are also

Felt-tip pens are the ideal way to ink your sketches. A fineliner, medium-tip pen and sign pen should meet all of your needs, whatever your style and preferred subjects. A few colored felt-tip pens can be a good addition to your kit, allowing you to introduce color at the inking stage.

very fast; they last a long time too. Otherwise, a handheld sharpener is fine. One that comes with a couple of spare blades can be a worthwhile investment, to ensure that your pencils are always sharp.

Along with a sharpener, you will need an eraser for removing any visible pencil lines from your inked sketches prior to coloring. Choose a high-quality eraser that does not smudge the pencil lead, scuff the paper, or leave dirty fragments all over your work. A soft "putty" eraser works best, since it absorbs pencil lead rather than just rubbing it away. For this reason, putty erasers do become dirty with use. Keep yours clean by trimming it carefully with scissors every now and then.

INKING PENS

The range of inking pens can be bewildering, but some basic rules will help you select the pens you need. Inked lines in most types of manga tend to be quite bold so buy a thin-nibbed pen, about 0.5 mm (.02 inches) and a medium-size nib, about 0.8 mm (.03 inches). Make sure that the ink in the pens is waterproof; this ink won't smudge or run. Next, you will need a medium-tip felt pen. Although you won't need to use this pen very often to ink the outlines of your characters, it is still useful for filling in small detailed areas of solid black. The Pentel sign pen does this job well. Last, consider a pen that can create different line widths according to the amount of pressure you put on the tip. These pens replicate brushes and allow you to create flowing lines such as those seen on hair and clothing. The Pentel brush pen does this very well, delivering a steady supply of ink to the tip from a replaceable cartridge.

Test-drive a few pens at your art store to see which ones suit you best. All pens should produce clean, sharp lines with a deep black pigment.

MARKERS AND COLORING AIDS

Many artists use markers, rather than paint, to color their artwork, because markers are easy to use and come in a huge variety of colors and shades. Good-quality markers, such as those made by Chartpak, Letraset, or Copic, produce excellent, vibrant results, allowing you to build up multiple layers of color so you can create

Markers come in a wide variety of colors, which allows you to achieve subtle variations in tone. In addition to a thick nib for broad areas of color, the Copic markers shown here feature a thin nib for fine detail.

rich, detailed work and precise areas of shading. Make sure that you use your markers with marker or layout paper to avoid bleeding. Markers are often refillable, so they last a long time. The downside is that they are expensive, so choose a limited number of colors to start with, and add as your needs evolve. As always, test out a few markers in your art store before buying any.

However, markers are not the only coloring media. Paints and gouache also produce excellent results, and can give your work a distinctive look. Add white gouache, which comes in a tube, to your work to create highlights and sparkles of light. Apply it in small quantities with a good-quality watercolor brush.

It is also possible to color your artwork on a computer. This is quick to do, although obviously there is a high initial cost. It also tends to produce flatter color than markers or paints.

DRAWING AIDS

Most of your sketching will be done freehand, but there are situations, especially with man-made objects such as the edges of buildings or the wheels of a car, when your line work needs to be crisp and sharp to create the right look. Rulers, circle guides, and compasses all provide this accuracy. Rulers are either metal or plastic; in most cases, plastic ones work best, though metal ones tend to last longer. For circles, use a circle guide, which is a plastic sheet with a wide variety of different-sized holes stamped out of it. If the circle you want to draw is too big for the circle guide, use a compass that can hold a pencil and inking pen.

A selection of warm and cool grays is a useful addition to your marker colors and most ranges feature several different shades. These are ideal for shading on faces, hair, and clothes.

MALE FRONT VIEW

When drawing a male face, the same basic rules apply as to the female, with some significant differences. The jawline is more chiseled, with sharper lines and a squared-off base. The eyes also may be slightly smaller than those of a female, the mouth slightly larger, and the neck wider.

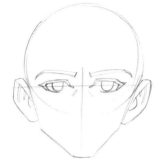

Start with an oval for the head, and bring this to a squared-off chin. Draw a central vertical line to help with positioning.

Draw a horizontal across the face and position the eyes across it. Add eyebrows above the eyes, and then position the ears using the same horizontal.

Use your vertical line as a guide for positioning the nose and mouth. Then sketch in a couple of lines to suggest the contours of the cheekbones.

Add hair. Draw spiky bangs across the front of the head. Then create the rest of the hair from a point on the crown out to the left and right.

Ink the main lines, working the hair as a single entity. Establish the eyebrows with two lines, and color the pupils black around the highlights.

Now add color. Use a pale pink for the face, with darker shadows in the ears. Give him pale blue eyes, and color the hair in two shades of brown.

MALE PROFILE

Here is the same face, but in profile. The features should all be in the same relative positions as in the front view. Note how the brow juts out above the eye, and the nose goes to a sharp point. The top lip should overhang the bottom slightly, and the jaw should step up in angles to the ear.

Start with a circle, then draw a rough triangle down to make a pointed chin. Add a vertical for the back of the neck.

Refine the profile, giving your figure a pointed nose, small mouth, and pointed chin.

Create a horizontal around which to position the visible eye and ear. Add a double line for the eyebrow, and a couple of lines to suggest the cheekbone.

Create the hair, working from a point on the crown forward and back to make a short, spiky, cropped style.

Ink the main lines of your sketch. Double-outline the eye, and draw the black pupil. Erase any pencil lines as you no longer need them.

His skin is pale pink, with darker beige areas of shadow in his ears, under the bangs, and under the chin. Color his hair using two shades of brown.

AN EAR IN DETAIL

As well as the overall face, it's worth taking a moment to look at how the individual features are constructed. The hardest of these is possibly the ear, as we spend the least time looking at it! Everyone's ears are different, but there are general features that you can use to make your character's ear look credible.

Start with two circles, one bigger than the other. Join them with a vertical line.

Refine the main outline of the ear, all around.

Echo this shape inside to create the fold of the ear. Then draw a semicircle and add some other detailing inside the ear.

Take the same ear and draw it from a three-quarter angle by compressing the whole shape sideways.

The profile of the ear from behind is simpler. Draw a narrow C-shape, with a line down it to create the fold at the edge of the ear. Add light shading.

SHORT CROP

Sometimes the most effective haircut can be the most simple. Here is a standard crop, very popular with trendy young males and also tough guys and gangsters. It's a simple shape following the contours of the hairline, and can be filled predominantly with black, but with a slight area of color if needed.

Create a basic head with two eyes, nose, mouth, and one ear. Draw a wavy line to indicate the front of the hairline.

From the end of the wavy line draw around the top of the head, down and along the ear, creating a sideburn, then work up to join the wavy line.

You have now created the basic outline of the hair, so ink over it.

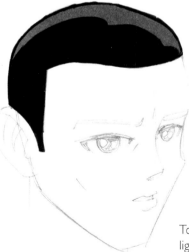

Draw a wavy line on the top of the head, to create a highlight, then ink the rest of the hair using black.

To finish, color the high-light on top of the head using gray.

SIDE PART

This is a casual style for an everyday manga male. A loose cut parted on one side, and hanging down behind the ears to the collar. This type of style is suitable for a range of characters, and has a cool, confident look about it.

Draw a basic head, with two eyes, nose, mouth, and an ear. Starting higher than the outline of the head, work a few long spiky lines across your head.

Now complete the outline of the hair. Start from the starting point above the head and work up and around, creating spikes as you go. Finish with a couple of spikes in front of the ear.

Create a couple of spiky strands on the right on the face, to complete the profile of the hair.

Start to ink, working all around the profile of the hair. Ink a couple of lines on top of the head to help with shape.

Define an area of highlight across the top of the head using a gray pen.

Leaving the highlight white, color the rest of the hair gray.

BLUE AND SPIKY

Here we have a more fashionable look, with a variety of spikes and strands going off in various directions. Spiky hair is a typical manga look, often in bright, vivid colors. This style is in a bold blue, and is cut long at the sides in a contemporary fashion. Practice in creating spiky styles is always worth it.

Start by drawing a basic head, with two eyes, nose, mouth, and one ear. Then, starting outside the head, draw some long, spiky points of hair across the face.

Add a couple of long points of hair in front of the ear. Then, again starting outside the head area, draw a couple of similar length points on the right.

From the same point as last time, work around the head, creating the profile of the hair. Echo the shape of the head, adding a couple of spikes on top.

Starting from where you made your first mark, ink the outline of the hair. Ink behind the bangs on the left-hand side so that the bangs look right.

Create an area of highlight across the top of the head using a fine blue pen.

Color the hair blue. As a finishing touch, indicate a couple of stray strands of hair across the highlight, using a fine pen.

RED WARRIOR PONYTAIL

Old-fashioned styles like this are used in more traditional manga stories of sword fighters and samurai warriors. The hair is worn long at the back, with lengthy bangs and sides. Some of the hair is collected up in a high topknot, which sits upright on the top of the head, before cascading down the back. It's a dramatic, bold style and is very effective in portraying fast movement.

Draw a basic head, with eyes, nose, mouth, and one ear. In front of the ear, add some long, thin strands of hair.

Starting at the crown, draw a line out to the side and down, and use this to start drawing spiky bangs to join your first long strands.

From the same start point, work a line over the crown and then create strands of hair behind the ear.

Now add a ponytail to the top of the head, held in place by a scrunchie. Take the ponytail to the same length as your longest spiked locks.

Ink around all the main lines of the hair, including all the spikes, the bangs and ponytail, and the scrunchie.

Create the outlines for two areas of highlight, one on top of the head, and one on the ponytail. Draw these using a fine red pen.

Leaving the highlights and the scrunchie white, color the hair bright red. Then color the underside of the ponytail and the tips of the hair with a darker shade of red.

FALLING BANGS

Large curtains like this are very popular in manga. This style is created from a basic center part, shoulder-length at the back, and brushed up into two dramatic bangs falling down on either side of the face. These are usually given shiny highlights to make them more emphatic and exaggerated.

Start by drawing a basic head, with eyes, nose, mouth, and one ear. Then draw the shape of a bird in flight, with the center line of your head at its center.

From each end of this line, draw a long curtain of spiky hair. Starting from the center line, draw jagged lines to meet the spiky curtains.

Next create the top of the hair, following the line of the top of the head, then draw some long strands down the back of the head on both sides.

Begin inking your hairstyle. Outline all the spikes and over the top of the head. Add a few wispy strands of hair from the center part.

Next create some areas of highlight on the spiky curtains of hair using a red-brown pen. Add one near the top and one in the middle of each.

Working around the white highlights, color your hairstyle reddish brown.

17

BLACK-AND-WHITE FASHIONISTA

Hairstyles can be very bold and creative in manga. This style is typical of a very fashionable youth-look, with asymmetrical spikes and a bold slash of white on the bangs. In what is essentially a black-and-white graphic medium, hairstyles like this are a useful way of making a character instantly identifiable.

Draw a basic head with eyes, nose, mouth, and one ear. Starting at the crown of the head, draw a curved line out and down, then four broad spikes, with a straight line back to the crown.

Starting about halfway down your last line, draw a spiky point over the left eye, then some longer spikes in front of the ear.

Add three large spikes on the crown, then draw down the back of the head behind the ear. Add a couple of horizontal spikes under the ear.

Ink all the main lines of the sketch. Make sure that the top area that you created first, on top of the head, reads as separate from the rest of the hairstyle.

Now start to color. Create some zigzags on the spikes on the left, and leave the area below white for now. Also leave the top area white. Color everything else black.

Color the spikes a dark gray, then add some touches of pale gray to the tips of the white hair.

BLACK PONYTAIL

This is a simple-looking ponytail, bunched at the back of the head. The cut is a basic, unremarkable style, and would probably suit a character unconcerned with fashion and trends, perhaps somebody from a rural background. The white highlight around the crown helps to emphasize the round shape of the haircut.

Draw a basic head with eyes, nose, mouth, and ear. Then, starting at the ear, draw spiky bangs. Continue the bangs well outside the head.

Starting where your last line finished, draw around the top of the head, adding three spikes at the crown, and continue your line down to the top of the ear.

Add a ponytail with a curly, flicked-up end flowing out behind the ear. Then indicate a spiky area of highlight on top of the head.

Ink around the profile of the hair, including the ponytail.

Now, using black, color your hairstyle. Leave the highlight you penciled white, coloring the top of the head. Leave some white flashes on the ponytail, then color it.

WILD PINK SPIKES

Here is a bold spiky look for a passionate, young male character. The spikes are jutting out in all directions like a flaming fire, and the color is eye-catching and dramatic. The style would suggest a fiery, passionate temperament.

Create a basic head with eyes, nose, mouth, and an ear. Starting in front of the ear, work across drawing a series of spikes for bangs. Continue this outside the area of the head.

Then, starting where you finished, work more large spikes right around the head, behind the ear, and down into the side of the neck.

Now draw a spiky halo on top of the head, within the outer ring of spikes. Put some on the crown, and bring some into the spikes of the bangs. Add a few spikes in between those on the top of the head.

Ink around both haloes of spikes. Then ink around the spikes you interspersed between those on top of the head.

Finally color your hairstyle a dramatic dark pink color. Where the top halo casts shadows on the rest of the hair, double up on color, or use a darker purple.

SIMPLE BLONDE

This is a neat, simple haircut for a nice, sensible character. It suggests honesty and openness, and could be used for a college student or sports star perhaps. It has a basic center part, and is cut to a loose collar-length at the back.

Create a basic head with eyes, nose, mouth, and one ear. Draw a center line from crown to forehead, then flick lines to the left and to the right.

Add a couple of lines on top of the ear. Then make a series of spikes between your single line and the ear. From the two lines draw down a few spikes of hair.

Start on the right, and create the top of the hair to the center line, then work down behind the ear, and draw three spikes beside the neck. Add a few lines on the right.

Ink the main lines of the hairstyle, including the center line so that the style reads as having a definite center part.

Now start to add color. Use a bright yellow for the top left area, then use a more golden tone for the top right and down the left-hand side. Color the spiky area on the right using brown.

21

MOHAWK

Punk styles are familiar to manga readers, and this is a good example of a striking cut that can make a character stand out from the crowd. The Mohawk is derived from Native Americans, but has become a fashion classic with the alternative youth cultures of the last few decades.

Draw a basic head with eyes, nose, mouth, and an ear. Start with a center line, then draw a series of upright lines from the middle of the hairline.

Create the profile of the Mohawk from the top of the uprights to the back of the head.

Add groups of three lines, working back along the center line. Note that the lines get shorter as you near the back of the head.

Ink the part, and then ink around the spiky profile of the hair and bangs.

Finally use two shades of green to color your hairstyle. Use a paler color in between the inked uprights, and a darker shade for the front of the Mohawk to give it width.

RED SWEPT-BACK

Not all manga hair has to fall down in front of the face. Here is a style swept up from the forehead in fiery red waves. It's cut high and short at the back to focus attention on the top, and a glossy white highlight gives dramatic visual impact.

Start by drawing a basic head with eyes, nose, mouth, and one ear. Then, starting from the ear, draw a series of short spikes across the forehead to indicate the hairline.

Next, starting where you finished, draw a series of large spikes over the top of the head, and down to the ear.

Now draw the outline of a highlight right across the top of the head.

Ink around the entire outline of the hairstyle.

Leaving the highlight white, color the hair bright red. Then add some darker red shadows on the points of the bangs, on the large spike behind the ear, and the hair in front of the ear.

PAGEBOY WITH BANGS

A traditional feudal-era style, this pageboy cut would be suitable for stories set in a bygone age. It's feminine by today's standards but very much a male cut in its own time. The highlights on the main hair body and the part give a healthy-looking sheen.

Draw a basic head with eyes, nose, mouth, and one ear. Starting from the ear, draw a line up and across the head, just above eye level. Continue it out beyond the line of the head.

From where you finished, draw the profile of the hairstyle, making it high and smooth. Take it down below the ear, and smooth into the neck. Add a similar piece on the right.

Next, chop the bangs into thick, fairly even chunks. Then outline a highlight across the top of the head. Make some of the highlight cut across the bangs.

Ink around the basic shape of the hairstyle, then ink around the highlight. Where this cuts across the bangs, do not ink so that the gaps remain in the bangs. Add a couple of inked lines in the highlight.

Finally, working around the outlined highlight and creating another one on the right of the part, color the hair black.

PROFILE HAND

Here is a basic hand in profile, with thumb and fingers all extended in a gentle curving pose. This hand shows the basic distance between the ball of the thumb and the back of the hand, and the relative length of the fingers. It could be reaching out to hold something or waving.

Start by drawing an eggcup shape, and add a curved line to close it across the top. Next draw two lines coming down for the wrist, and add a short center line parallel to them.

Draw two ovals, one for the pad and one for the top of the thumb, and join with a curved line. Then draw two circles on the opposite side of the palm, and join with curved lines.

Now flesh out the thumb and first finger by joining the ovals and circles you have made.

Add three more fingers of different sizes. Indicate nails on the thumb and fingers. Go over the main lines to give them greater definition, and shade the palm and inner fingers.

25

OPEN HAND

This is a standard open-palm view with all fingers extended and parallel to each other. It shows clearly the basic shapes of the hand, and is a good starting point. You can see how the ball of the thumb takes up one side of the palm, with a similar shape on the opposite side. There is also a distinct line where the fingers begin. Each finger is clearly divided into three segments.

Draw an eggcup shape for the palm and close its top with a curved line. Bisect it vertically with a line, and add two curved lines to indicate the wrist.

Take a slightly curved line out to the right. Draw a curved line into the palm and about two-thirds up your thumb line. Add a small semicircle next to this.

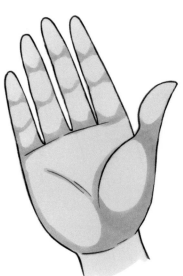

Draw two fingers on either side of your center line. Keep them in the correct proportion with one another and give each two joints. Use your own hand for reference.

Ink around the outside of the hand and add creases on the palm, across the wrist, and at the base of the fingers. Color your hand pink.

Start to build up areas of shadow using orange-brown. Shadows form around the joints, at the base of the palm and along its creases, and up into the thumb.

TENSE HAND

You can see here how the finger joints operate. Beginning with the knuckles, each joint folds in on itself until the hand becomes a closed ball. The fingers here are not clenched tightly enough to make a fist, but show a degree of tension.

Start with an eggcup shape, with one side longer than the other. Close the top with a curved line. Add a center line at the base of the palm, and lines for the wrist.

Draw four circles across your top line: these will be the knuckle joints. Now add a line from each circle to give you the outer line of each finger.

Add an ellipse to the end of each line and use these to position the first joint of each finger. Add a second joint to the finger closest to you.

Refine the main lines of your hand and fingers, and add a nail to the closest finger. Then indicate the creases on the back of the hand.

Ink in all your main lines, around the wrist, palm, and all the fingers. Ink the creases on the back of the hand and on the finger joints you can see.

CLENCHED FIST

A very useful pose, particularly in action manga, is the closed fist. Here you can see a view looking down on the back of the hand, and you can see clearly the tensed-up sinews that connect the muscle to the bone. The knuckles are clearly indicated at the top of the shape.

Draw an eggcup shape at a 45° angle. Then draw two lines down from it to make a wrist. Close off the top with a curved line, then sketch in a center line up from the wrist.

Create basic shapes for the knuckles by drawing four circles. Make the middle two butt up against the curved line; the first and last should sit across it.

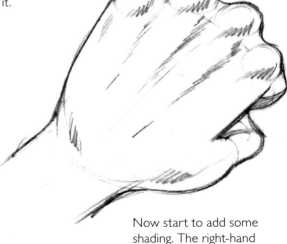

Define the thumb with two semicircles and a triangle, then create two joints for the index finger. Then outline around the whole hand.

Now start to add some shading. The right-hand side of each knuckle is in shadow, as is the base of the thumb. There is also shading around the wrist area.

CLAWING HAND

The hand is a tool that can be used for many different purposes. This is a clutching pose, which is good for gripping, climbing, holding, and similar purposes. The index finger and the thumb are the principal levers, with the remaining fingers used for added grip. You can see how the fingers are folded at the joints, indicated by the darker tones.

Draw a U-shape and close off the top with a curved line. Add verticals top and bottom, then draw two short lines to create the wrist.

Add an oval, overlapping the right-hand edge of the palm, the whole length of the palm. Add the top joint of the thumb across the oval.

Draw the outer edge of the index finger, then create the fingers from a series of ovals and U shapes, butting to this line.

Ink around the edge of the hand, and around the individual fingers and thumb. Add ink, too, to the base of the thumb, the base of the first finger, and the wrist.

Now add a flat color over the whole hand. In this case, a pale pink was used.

Add some shading to those areas that are in shadow. These include the base of the hand, the tops of the fingers, the base of the index finger, and parts of the thumb.

PUNCHING FIST

This is a more dramatic view of a fist, which is coming towards the viewer. It shows how compact and tightly closed the fingers are, with the thumb tucked underneath to prevent any damage. You can see the shading indicating the knuckles across the top of the shape.

Begin by drawing a rectangle with one end smaller than the other and a curved upperside. The top line will become the line of the knuckles.

Draw three lines up from the bottom, stopping about three-quarters of the way up. Fill the gaps between them with a series of four ellipses.

Add an oval shape to the bottom right-hand corner, then sketch the last joint of the thumb which folds over the oval. Round off the bases of the fingers.

Redefine the main lines, creating definite gaps between the fingers and shadow at their bases. Then indicate shading on the palm and add a thumbnail.

Now ink the sketch. Ink around the outside of the hand, then ink the gaps between the fingers and the finger joints. Finally, ink around the thumbnail.

CONTROLLED DETERMINATION

The average arm falls down to just below the hip. The pose here shows an arm and clenched fist held down by the side in a manner that suggests the figure is controlling his emotions. The position of the hip and buttocks counterbalances the arm and the forward leaning stance.

Draw two circles. Add a large ellipse, then butt the base of a triangle to it. Connect the two circles and the ellipse, and the two circles and the triangle.

Flesh out the arm from shoulder to elbow and elbow to wrist. Using the triangle as the palm of the hand, add a thumb and two finger joints to it.

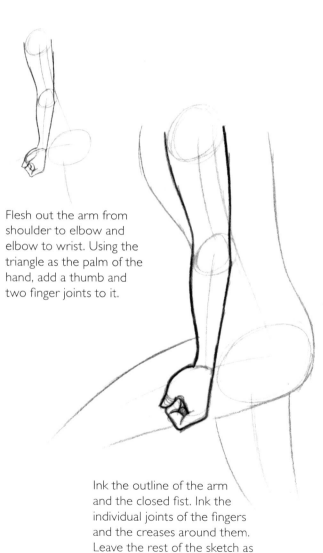

Add a suggestion of a body to which the arm is attached. The spine runs parallel to the arm down to the ellipse. One leg is straight, the other steps forward.

Ink the outline of the arm and the closed fist. Ink the individual joints of the fingers and the creases around them. Leave the rest of the sketch as pencil only.

GRASPING AT YOU

This is a good dynamic action pose, where the hand is clutching toward the viewer with an arm bent at the elbow. It involves foreshortening, as the forearm is pointing horizontally toward you, rendering it as an oval shape behind the hand.

Slightly overlap two ovals, then draw a third a little distance away. This is the shoulder joint. Draw a line to attach this to one of the ovals: this is the foreshortened lower arm.

Draw four circles along the edge of the oval: these are the first finger joints. Now create the two upper joints of each finger: these are roughly equal in length when viewed from this angle.

Add an ellipse to create the pad of the thumb, and join this to the hand with two curved lines.

Ink the main lines, including the creases around the top joint of each finger and under the pad of the thumb.

POINTING FINGER

A pointing hand can be very useful in a manga story. Here you can see how the index finger is stretched out in a straight line, with the remaining fingers folded back into the palm. The thumb is stretched out diagonally away from the hand in this case, although it can also be tucked away as in the fist pose.

Draw an upside-down U-shape, closing off the open end with a curved line. This is the back of the hand. Add two lines for the wrist, and a center line.

Create the knuckles by drawing four circles across the back of the hand. Draw a short line at the side of the first three, with a longer one beside the fourth.

Join the three short lines with curved lines for the joints of the first three fingers. Add the pointing index finger with its joints, then add a thumb.

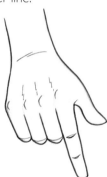

Ink around the main lines of the wrist, hand, fingers, and thumb. Add creases to the wrist and back of the hand, as well as to the knuckle and finger joints.

Leaving the knuckles white, add a flat color to the rest of the hand, fingers, and thumb.

Now create areas of shading. The left-hand side of the wrist is in shadow, as are the bent fingers, the left of the thumb, and the joints of the index finger.

GRIPPING HAND

A gripping hand can be applied to any object from a sword to a tennis racquet. The hand here is grasping a handle or hilt of some kind. The index finger is slightly extended beyond the rest of the fingers, which is a natural position and gives extra control. The tip of the thumb can be seen curving round behind the handle.

Draw two ellipses at right angles to each other. Bisect the larger with a circle, then add two more circles. Join the three circles with a curved line, and draw two straight lines, one on each side of the smaller ellipse.

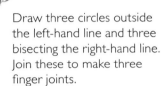

Draw three circles outside the left-hand line and three bisecting the right-hand line. Join these to make three finger joints.

Create the index finger by fleshing out the first three circles you drew. Leave a gap between the index finger and the other three. Then add the thumb.

Ink around the wrist, hand, fingers, and thumb. Add some shading around the joints. To finish, strengthen the baton the hand is holding, adding shading.

FINGER ON THE TRIGGER

This pose shows how to hold the stock of a weapon while keeping a finger on the trigger. The important thing here is to visualize the weapon handle when you draw the hand, otherwise the grip will look unnatural. Note how the three remaining fingers fold down around the stock.

Draw an ellipse, and add two curved lines for a wrist. Draw four circles, one overlapping the ellipse, two inside it, and the last protruding only a little. Add a short line out from the top circle.

The four circles are knuckle joints. From the lower three, draw finger joints. From the line at the top, draw the rounded joint of the index finger. Draw the fold of skin between the two fingers.

Now get an indication of the weapon that the hand is holding. This has a base under the fingers, together with the trigger and a suggestion of the barrel. This does not need to be detailed.

Ink the hand to emphasize it. Ink around the wrist, sides, and individual fingers. Ink the joints, and define the knuckles.

Now add a flat color over the hand. In this sketch, a pale pink has been used.

Add some shading to those areas that need it. These are the underside of the wrist and hand, and the finger joints.

FOLDED ARMS

One of the hardest things to get right is a pair of folded arms. It can be a dramatic visual example of body language in a manga story, and makes a character look firm and immovable. You can see how the chest is arched backward slightly to exaggerate the gesture.

Create shoulder and elbow joints by drawing four circles, one at each corner of an imaginary square. Join the top three with straight lines, and add a center line. Draw a line from each elbow across the chest.

Flesh out the upper and lower arms by joining the joints. The lower arms are folded, so draw one on top of the other. Indicate a torso.

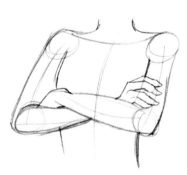

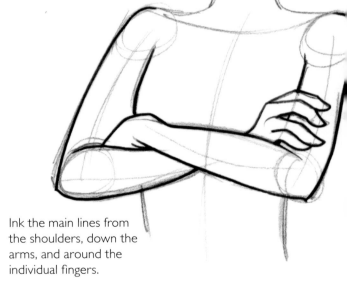

Add shoulders and a suggestion of a neck. Then work on the hands. The left hand has no detail. Add four jointed fingers to the right hand, above the elbow.

Ink the main lines from the shoulders, down the arms, and around the individual fingers.

GALLERY

pointing

right The index finger points and the rest of the fingers are folded. The tip of the thumb peeps out.

gripping thumb

below With a thick accessory like a book, the thumb joint comes to the forefront. Only part of the palm and first finger are visible in this type of grip.

spread fingers

below This is a good neutral pose. Note that the shadows are on the right of the hand, in between the fingers, and to the right of all the knuckle joints.

holding

above In a holding pose, the thumb disappears, the index finger sticks out, and the knuckles form a sloping line.

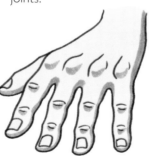

semi-open

above In this pose, the fingers point, but in a far less aggressive manner than in other poses. The hand here is also more relaxed.

fingertip hold

below Finger and thumb come together to hold a fine item like a drinking straw. Take care with details such as the fingernails.

gripping fist

above When the fist is tightly closed around a staff or other weapon, the knuckles are prominent. A small area of thumb shows.

sword fight

right A closed-fist grip is used to hold weapons. Whoosh lines give the sensation of speed to static objects like swords.

two-fisted

below Action manga can involve holding all kinds of weapons. The hands are gripping tightly, giving strong highlights on the knuckles and dark shadows under the folded fingers.

punching

above This fist is pushing upward. Strong, dynamic coloring produces dark shadows and bright highlights.

THREE-QUARTER VIEW

From another angle, you can see how the toes are used to balance the weight of the foot, and how the arch is used to direct the movement of the tread. The ankle here is sharply defined with strong shadows.

Draw a triangle with rounded sides, then a straight line to represent the leg. At this stage, make three lines for the foot.

Flesh out the leg and foot. Draw verticals up from the triangle to make the leg. Then draw from the triangle down to make the foot. Block in the line of the toes.

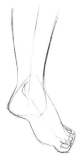

Create the ankle joint, then add the toes. Indicate toenails.

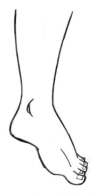

Ink the outline of the leg and foot. Then ink the ankle joint and the line of the instep. Ink the toes separately, then ink the individual toenails.

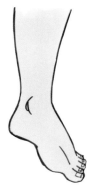

Color the leg and foot; here a flat pale pink was used.

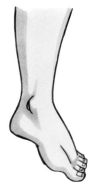

Then introduce shading and modeling, using a dark beige, on the left of the leg, around the ankle, and under the foot.

STEPPING LEG

Now try drawing this leg, which is bent slightly at the knee in a forward stepping position, with the foot flat on the floor and ready to take the weight of the body as it moves forward. Note how the shin is relatively flat while the calf behind curves out to contain the muscle.

Start by drawing basic shapes: an ellipse for the knee joint and a wedge for the foot. Draw a line from the apex of the triangle to the center of the ellipse, and another from the top of the ellipse up.

Now flesh out the leg. Add two lines down to the knee to create the thigh, then work down, tapering in to the ankle.

Start to add more detail. Redefine the kneecap. Then, refine the foot, giving it a clear profile and outlining the big toe. Draw a triangle to suggest the ankle bone.

Ink the outline of the leg and foot. Then ink the kneecap and ankle bone. Finally, suggest some of the other toes.

Now get some color into your sketch. In this case, a flat pale pink was used.

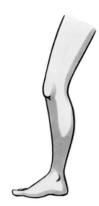

Finally use a dark beige for modeling and shading. There is shading down the back of the leg and on the shin, around the kneecap, and under the foot.

SOLE OF THE FOOT

To understand the structure of the foot, it's a good idea to study the sole and see how the various parts relate to each other. Here you can see clearly the different widths of the ball and heel, and the descending position and size of the toes.

Draw an egg shape to represent the heel and an irregular ellipse for the ball of the foot. Join them with a curved line.

Join the two basic shapes to create the profile of the sole.

Now add the toes along the curved line that forms the top of the foot: the big toe is an ellipse, the others are rounder.

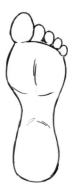

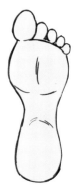

Ink the main lines of your sketch. Ink the outline of the foot as well as the individual toes. Ink a suggestion of the ball of the foot and the heelpad.

Color the entire foot using a flat pale pink.

Now get some shading into the foot. The bases of the toes are in shadow, as is the area of the arch and part of the heelpad.

STANDING LEG, FRONT VIEW

From the front, the leg is a much narrower shape. It should taper in at the knee and again at the ankle before spreading out at the foot. Note how the kneecap sits centrally about halfway up the leg, and protrudes from the middle.

Draw a rough circle for a kneecap, with a triangle with a curved base for a foot. Add two verticals for the leg.

Now flesh out the leg. Add a line going into the knee, out again for the calf, and tapering into the ankle on both sides of the leg.

Redefine the kneecap, then work on the foot. Draw circles for the toes, and define the profile of the sole.

Ink the outline of the leg, defining the ankle, heel, and toes. Ink the kneecap, and add a couple of lines for the front of the ankle.

Now add color. Here a flat pale pink has been used over the whole leg and foot.

Use shading to get some modeling into the leg. There are shadows down the left of the leg and under the knee at the front. Suggest shading on the toes.

UTILITY BOOT

This is a robust-looking functional boot, with a practical flat sole and reinforced toe and heel parts. It would be suitable for a military uniform or for a motorcycle rider, and would suit either a male or female foot. The loose folds around the lip indicate that the trousers are tucked inside the boot.

Draw a circle for the knee and a triangle for the foot. Join these with a vertical and add another vertical for the upper leg.

Create the basic shape of the three-quarter boot.

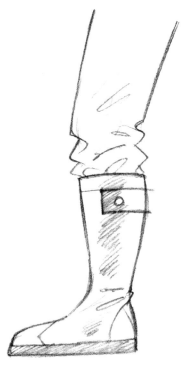

Now add the trouser-covered leg, with fabric bunching around the knee and tucked into the boot.

Define the sole, heel guard, and toecap of the boot, and add some detailing to the top.

Build up some shading on the boot. Shade the sole and around the middle of the side to round out the shape, making the boot look more realistic.

TREKKING BOOT

Using a stepping-off foot position as a base, this sturdy walking boot has a firm toecap and six-eyehole laces. The sole has a deep functional tread, ideal for all-terrain exploring or simple urban streets. Note how the heel is deeper than the rest of the sole, which gives the foot extra support where it's needed.

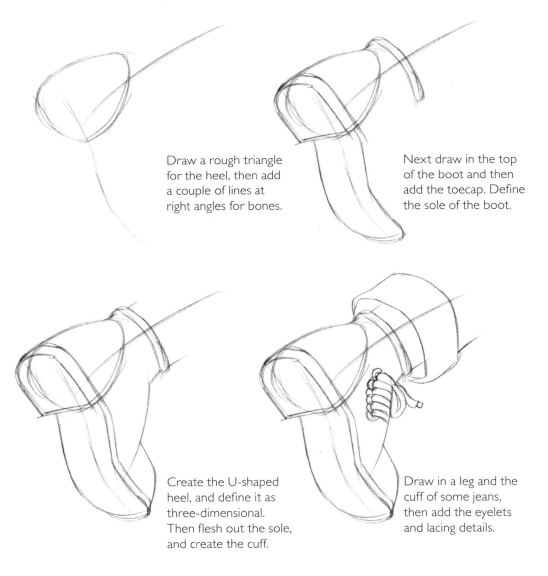

Draw a rough triangle for the heel, then add a couple of lines at right angles for bones.

Next draw in the top of the boot and then add the toecap. Define the sole of the boot.

Create the U-shaped heel, and define it as three-dimensional. Then flesh out the sole, and create the cuff.

Draw in a leg and the cuff of some jeans, then add the eyelets and lacing details.

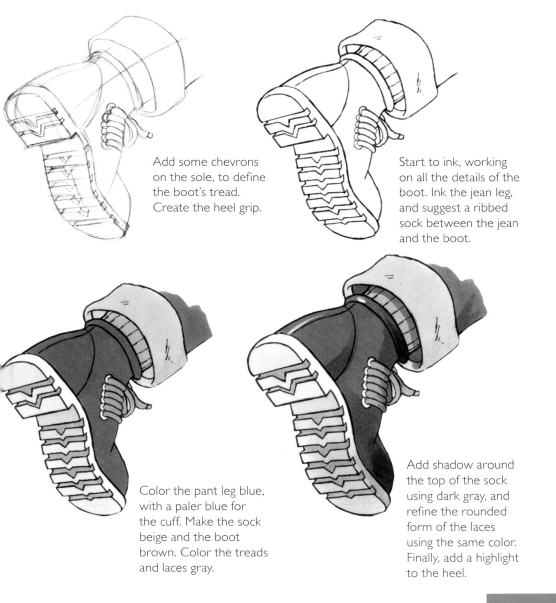

Add some chevrons on the sole, to define the boot's tread. Create the heel grip.

Start to ink, working on all the details of the boot. Ink the jean leg, and suggest a ribbed sock between the jean and the boot.

Color the pant leg blue, with a paler blue for the cuff. Make the sock beige and the boot brown. Color the treads and laces gray.

Add shadow around the top of the sock using dark gray, and refine the rounded form of the laces using the same color. Finally, add a highlight to the heel.

SENSIBLE LACE-UP

This is a typical shoe for a male businessman. It's a traditional-looking lace-up shoe with toe and heel areas clearly defined. The heel is slightly deeper than the main sole, but not by much. The laces are tied in two loops in the normal manner. It's well worth looking at a pair of real laces to help you to get this drawing correct.

Draw two roughly triangular shapes and join them together with an angled line.

Join the triangles together with a double line, to create the sole, then add a heel. Create the upper from a curved line.

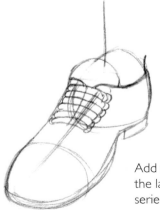

Add the eyelets and then the laces, which are a series of parallel lines.

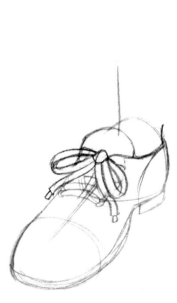

Sketch the heelguard, then create a bow for the lace.

Add a trouser leg and the suggestion of a ribbed sock. Create some shading on the pant leg, then on the upper of the shoe.

SMART SUIT

Every man must have a suit in his wardrobe. This manga male is wearing a typical two-piece suit and loafers. Note how the creases on each leg are clearly indicated, and how the jacket goes in at the waist to give a tailored look. The outfit is finished off with a folded handkerchief in the breast pocket.

Draw a basic figure using lines for bones, circles for joints, and triangles for pelvis and feet. Give him some hair. Add the top of a jacket, to waist level, then draw in the lapels. Add a collar and tie.

Add sleeves from the shoulders, down over the elbow joints. Add the rest of the jacket over the pelvis. Include patch pockets and a single button. Indicate creasing around the waist.

Next add trousers and shoes. Then finish off the figure's arms by adding hands.

Refine the lines of the collar and tie, then shade the tie. Add a handkerchief in the top pocket.

Ink all the main lines of your suit, shirt and tie, and shoes. Also ink the lines of the creases in the jacket and trousers.

MARTIAL ARTS

This is a typical martial arts suit, known as a *karategi*, or "gi" for short. It consists of a kimono top and *dogi* pants. The gi is loose-fitting to allow freedom of movement, and tied at the waist with a belt. The color of the belt denotes the grade, or skill-level, of the wearer. The character shown here has a black belt, which means he has achieved the highest grade of training (black belts themselves are further graded in levels known as first *dan*, second dan, third dan, and so on).

Start with a basic stick figure with lines for bones, circles for joints, and triangles for pelvis and feet. Draw the top of the jacket, down to the waist. Add the trim around the neck, and the belt at the waist.

Next, give him some baggy pants to just below knee level, then give your character legs and feet: there is no footwear in this costume.

Draw the rest of the jacket, then work on the details of the belt. Next draw the sleeves and give the figure hands. Draw in some creases at the elbows.

Now ink over the main lines, including the creases around the elbows, into the waist, and on the pants. Color the belt black, along with the insides of the sleeves and the shadow at the neckline.

STREET GEAR

For a cool-looking youth, try this bolero-length jacket and slim pants. The collar is worn up to convey attitude, and the shoulders are cut wide for a masculine feel. The white pants are slightly flared at the bottom, and have a narrow belt for contrast.

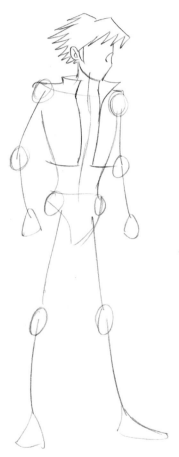

Next draw in the sleeves, with some creasing around the elbows, and add his hands. Indicate trim along the zipper and breast pockets.

Draw a basic stick figure with lines for bones, circles for joints, and triangles for pelvis and feet. Start with his bolero jacket, detailing the stand-up collar.

Add some trousers, with a flat waistband, then pocket details, and flared legs. Add his t-shirt, and give him shoes.

Finally, add some gray shading to the pants to give a more rounded look, and then add some thin white highlights on the shoulders.

Ink the main lines of the costume, including the creases, and shoes. Erase any pencil lines.

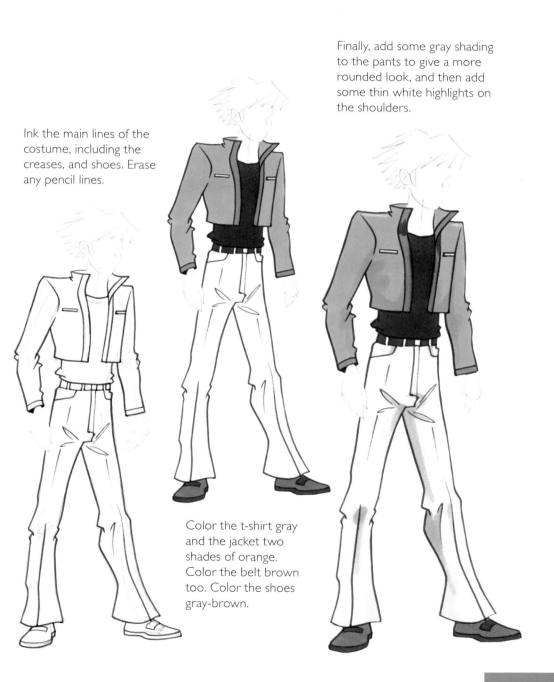

Color the t-shirt gray and the jacket two shades of orange. Color the belt brown too. Color the shoes gray-brown.

MILITARY GREATCOAT

Here's a much heavier look for a sci-fi or period story. The broad cuffs and collar have a military look, with a double-breasted front and a narrow belt at the waist. The boots are sturdy-looking and reinforced with steel. The yellow neckerchief gives a dashing touch of color to the coat, which is a drab, somber green.

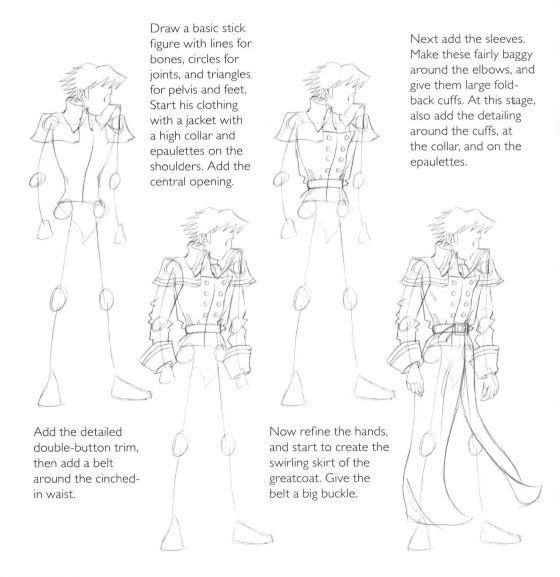

Draw a basic stick figure with lines for bones, circles for joints, and triangles for pelvis and feet. Start his clothing with a jacket with a high collar and epaulettes on the shoulders. Add the central opening.

Next add the sleeves. Make these fairly baggy around the elbows, and give them large fold-back cuffs. At this stage, also add the detailing around the cuffs, at the collar, and on the epaulettes.

Add the detailed double-button trim, then add a belt around the cinched-in waist.

Now refine the hands, and start to create the swirling skirt of the greatcoat. Give the belt a big buckle.

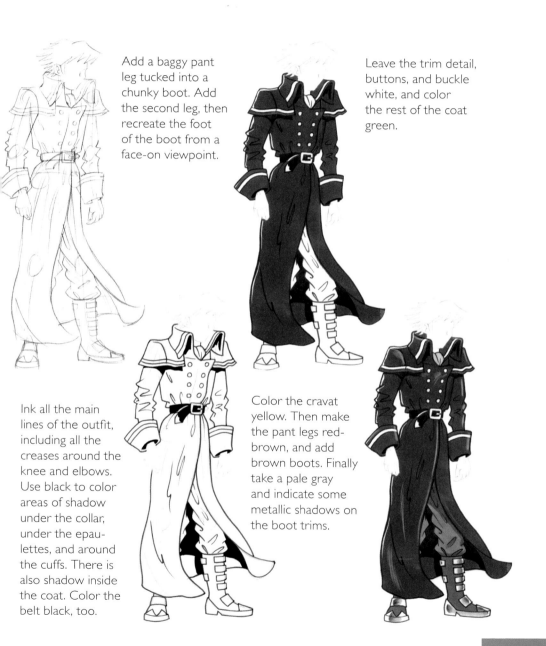

Add a baggy pant leg tucked into a chunky boot. Add the second leg, then recreate the foot of the boot from a face-on viewpoint.

Leave the trim detail, buttons, and buckle white, and color the rest of the coat green.

Ink all the main lines of the outfit, including all the creases around the knee and elbows. Use black to color areas of shadow under the collar, under the epaulettes, and around the cuffs. There is also shadow inside the coat. Color the belt black, too.

Color the cravat yellow. Then make the pant legs red-brown, and add brown boots. Finally take a pale gray and indicate some metallic shadows on the boot trims.

LEATHER JACKET AND JEANS

This is a typical street biker look, with traditional leather jacket and scruffy pants. Note the lapel shape of the jacket, with studs and shoulder and wrist tabs. The pockets are diagonal slits with dangling fasteners, and there is a waistband. The character is also wearing fingerless leather gloves with vents on the back of the hand.

Draw a basic stick figure with lines for bones, circles for joints, and triangles for pelvis and feet. Add an open neck jacket to slightly below waist level.

Add double lapels with a button trim detail.

Now add loose baggy sleeves, and give the character gloved hands. Add the neck detailing of the t-shirt.

Draw pants, fitting at the waist, with some creases around the knees and baggy at the bottom. Then draw athletic shoes, and add a belt at the waist.

Ink the t-shirt, jacket, pants, gloves, and athletic shoes. Ink detail on the lapels, the chest, at the waist, and around the cuffs. Color the belt black; leave the buckle white.

THERMAL JUMPSUIT

Here is a futuristic-looking jumpsuit made of thermal all-weather material. The black bands indicate strapping and may be used for support or for attachments. The elbows are reinforced with heavyweight padding, and the soles are flat and functional. An outfit like this could be worn by itself or underneath a bulkier outfit such as a spacesuit or battlesuit.

Create a basic stick figure with lines for bones, circles for joints, and triangles for pelvis and feet. Add a fitted top down to the waist. Then, flesh out both arms, and add hands.

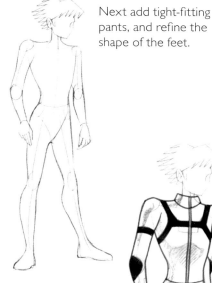

Next add tight-fitting pants, and refine the shape of the feet.

Add a neck trim and front fastening detail. Then add some detail on the bodice and around the arms and legs, then add elbow patches. Then draw in the soles and add toecap details to the shoes.

Ink the main lines of the costume, then use black to color the trim and detailing. Finally use gray to get some shading and modeling into the costume, and to suggest that it has a shiny surface texture.

TECH BATTLE ARMOR

You can have a lot of fun with this kind of armor, adding attachments and items at random for a busy, technological feel. There is some visible weaponry on the right shoulder, with what looks like a cannon blaster of some sort. The antenna on the left shoulder suggests a communication device or transmitter, and the boots look rugged and heavy-duty.

Start by drawing a basic figure with lines and circles for bones and joints, and triangles for pelvis and feet. Add a breast-plate, down to a fitted waist.

Turn to the pant details, sharpening the triangle of the pelvis and dividing it in two. Add kneepads, then start to detail the chunky boots.

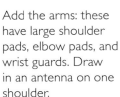

Add the arms: these have large shoulder pads, elbow pads, and wrist guards. Draw in an antenna on one shoulder.

Ink all the main lines and details. Then color black those areas that are not covered by protectors: the arms, torso, and the tops of the legs, leaving the details white.

Start to add shading to indicate a metallic finish to the protective shoulder, elbow and wrist pads, to the breastplate, to the pants, and to the boots.

Refine and sharpen the shading on the protective plates.

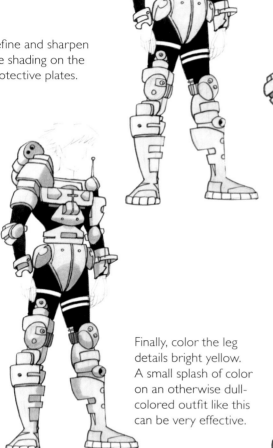

Finally, color the leg details bright yellow. A small splash of color on an otherwise dull-colored outfit like this can be very effective.

MONK ROBES

Priests and monks play a big part in many manga stories. This outfit consists of a plain brown under-robe, on top of which is worn a long flowing red robe, which is wrapped around the neck and shoulder before being tied at the waist, and hangs down to below the knee.

Create a basic figure using lines for bones, circles for joints, and triangles for pelvis and feet. Add a flowing sash over one shoulder and round the torso.

Draw the neckline with folds and creases, then add large flowing sleeves encasing the hands. Refine the waistline with a couple of horizontals.

From the waistline, create a full-length gathered double-skirt. Add a knotted sash at the waist. Finally at this stage, add flip-flops to the feet.

Ink all the main lines, trying to keep as many folds and creases in the drawing as you can: note there are creases around the elbows too. Then, color the inside of the sleeves black, as these areas are in shadow.

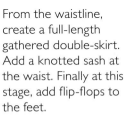

Color the left shoulder, sleeves, and under-robe using a flat dark brown.

Add color to the top robe using bright red, to give a nice contrast to the dull brown beneath.

Double up on color in the folds and creases to add greater realism. The folds on the top, around the waist, and on the skirt all need refining.

SWASHBUCKLING SWORDSMAN

Romantic tales of heroism and romance are very popular in manga. Here is an example of a typical dashing swordsman, with his graceful billowing blouse-top and tight-leg pants set off by a scarlet sash at the waist. His sword hangs at his side in a brown leather scabbard.

Start with the basic figure lines, then draw in a high collar top with billowing sleeves that go to tight frilled cuffs.

Draw a wide sash at the waist, with horizontal lines to show creases in the fabric.

Next draw in some slim-leg pants, ending in a slight flare midway down the calf. Draw some boots with a thin sole and slight heel.

Add a sword, slung down by the waist on a diagonal strap, and finish the drawing with a double-breasted flap on the front of the top.

Ink the main lines on your drawing, carefully indicating creases and folds on the top and at the groin.

Color the pants dark gray, and the sash bright red. Use a beige color to indicate shadows and folds on the white top, then color the scabbard brown, and the sword hilt gray-green.

Add some shadows to the pants with darker grays, and give the boots mauve shadows. Strengthen the beige shadows on the top with slightly darker shades.

SOLDIER

Occasionally manga tales may involve more realistic or contemporary military scenes. Army uniforms tend to follow a pattern such as that seen on this character. He's wearing a camouflaged battle uniform with helmet and utility belt, along with a backpack and sleeping roll. Below the knees he is wearing some strapping, known as puttees. This is a piece of cloth wrapped tightly round the calf from ankle to knee, and used as support.

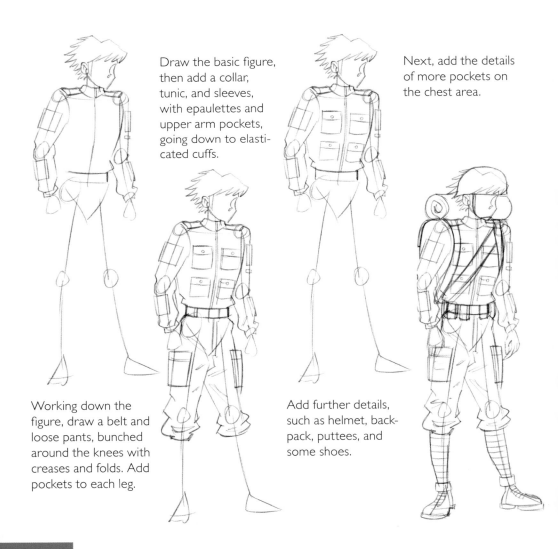

Draw the basic figure, then add a collar, tunic, and sleeves, with epaulettes and upper arm pockets, going down to elasticated cuffs.

Next, add the details of more pockets on the chest area.

Working down the figure, draw a belt and loose pants, bunched around the knees with creases and folds. Add pockets to each leg.

Add further details, such as helmet, backpack, puttees, and some shoes.

Now ink all the main lines and details of your drawing, using fineline pens as needed.

Color the basic uniform a yellow-green, and the puttees a dull ocher color, then color the boots brown.

Use a beige color on the bedroll and backpack, then add some dark-gray shading to the uniform in splotches.

Darken the center of the camouflage marks to give a more dynamic finish, and add some gray shading to the chest strap.

SPACESUIT

Here's a heavy-looking outfit designed to take the rigors of space travel, and possibly combat. The suit is extremely thick and has smooth curves to avoid radar detection. The surface of the suit is covered in a network of optical filaments and superconductors, which can help to disseminate friction when travelling at extreme speed.

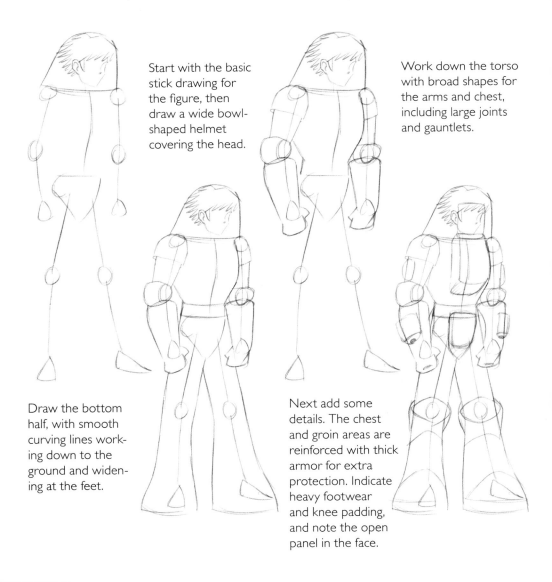

Start with the basic stick drawing for the figure, then draw a wide bowl-shaped helmet covering the head.

Work down the torso with broad shapes for the arms and chest, including large joints and gauntlets.

Draw the bottom half, with smooth curving lines working down to the ground and widening at the feet.

Next add some details. The chest and groin areas are reinforced with thick armor for extra protection. Indicate heavy footwear and knee padding, and note the open panel in the face.

Ink all your outside lines, and the important inside ones, before removing pencil marks.

Color the entire suit using a light gray. At this stage, you can leave slight white highlights where necessary.

Darken the shadows on your suit and note how the glass visor is dark gray to reflect sunlight.

Finally, use a process blue pencil and a little paint to indicate the network of circuitry on the suit. A couple of small red lights may be useful for visual interest.

STREET FIGHTER

After military fighters, sword-fighters, and space-age fighters, it's back down to earth with a street fighter, who fights in secret bouts using similar skills but not knowing much about his opponent. The vest is torn at the sleeves, and he wears wristbands and a headband together with an arm strap for maximum effect.

Starting with the basic figure, add a curving waistline and a V-shaped neck.

Now draw fastenings on the front of the tunic, and add some sweatbands on his wrists. Sketch martial arts slippers.

Next add some baggy, loose pants with elasticated cuffs. Indicate some creases at the groin area.

Finish up with a headband and arm strapping, together with some neck pendants.

Ink your drawing carefully, using fine black pens.

Color the tunic dark blue, and use pale blue-gray to put shadows on the white pants. The headband, wristbands, arm strap, and shoes should all be black.

Finally, darken and strengthen your shadows to give your drawing added impact.

space warrior

above This is a suit designed for hostile environments, with thick protection for the body, arms, and legs, heavy boots, and a gas tank on the back.

skater kid

right A hoodie, baggie pants, and thick crepe soles are typical clothing for skater kids. Ink and shading suggest the folds and creases in the fabric.

urban warrior

above A tight-fitting vest and pants emphasize the character's muscular physique. Wrist strappings reinforce the no-holds-barred attitude.

martial arts

right Based on a martial arts uniform, this black suit is great for someone who has to move freely, as this character must do to dodge the *shuriken* stars.

eco fighter

below Pants and tunic, high boots, thick belt, and a warm cloak, all in earth colors, are suitable for an eco warrior.

young warrior

left A simple outfit of pants tucked into boots, tunic, and scarf is ideal for a young warrior. These clothes offer freedom of movement to wield the staff.

GLOSSARY

apex The highest or culminating point.

asymmetrical Not symmetrical, or not the same on both sides.

bisect To divide into two usually equal parts.

bolero A loose waist-length jacket open at the front.

chevron A figure, pattern, or object having the shape of a V or an inverted V.

chiseled Formed or crafted as if with a chisel.

compass An instrument for describing circles or transferring measurements that consists of two pointed branches joined at the top by a pivot.

compress To press or squeeze together.

contours An outline, especially of a curving or irregular figure.

cravat A band or scarf worn around the neck.

dan The grade of training a martial artist has achieved.

disseminate To disperse throughout.

dogi The pants of a judo or karate uniform.

elasticated Containing strips of elastic in order to make the clothing fit snugly.

ellipse A closed plane curve resulting from the intersection of a circular cone and a plane cutting completely through it.

epaulettes Something that ornaments or protects the shoulder.

feudal Of or relating to a period in the Middle Ages.

foreshorten To shorten or make more compact.

gi A loose-fitting garment that allows freedom of movement.

gouache An opaque watercolor prepared with gum.

hilt A handle, especially of a sword or dagger.

manga A type of Japanese art used to tell stories in the form of comic books.

nib The sharpened point of a pen or marker.

opaque Something that cannot be seen through.

protrude To cause to project.

puttee A strip of cloth wound around the leg to form a legging, used by soldiers in World War I.

samurai A type of Japanese warrior.

scabbard A sheath for a sword or dagger.

taper To become progressively smaller toward one end.

FOR MORE INFORMATION

Anime and Manga Club
University of Massachusetts Amherst
41 Campus Center Way
Amherst, MA 01003
(413) 545-0306
Web site: http://www.umass.edu/rso/umjams
The University of Massachusetts Anime and Manga Club
is a group of manga enthusiasts who meet weekly
to discuss and swap anime and manga comics. They
hold annual events like the AnimeFirst! Marathon
and the twice yearly AniBreak. Both events are
devoted to watching and understanding the Japanese
comic art forms.

Japanese Eternal Trade Organization (JETRO)
1221 Avenue of the Americas
McGraw-Hill Building, 42nd Floor
New York, NY 10020
(212) 997-0400
Web site: http://www.jetro.org
The JETRO includes reports on Japanese culture and art,
especially the internationally well-known arts of Japanese
manga and anime. The JETRO publishes an annual report

each year on the Japanese anime market that can be accessed from their Web site.

Kyoto Seika University
Department of Story Manga
137 Kino-cho Iwakura
Sakyo-ku, Kyoto 606-8588
Japan
+81 75-702-5199
Web site: http://www.kyoto-seika.ac.jp/eng
Kyoto Seika University has an entire department devoted to the study of comic art and manga. The courses in the program emphasize international and historical perspectives, as well as teaching traditional techniques and styles to perfect the art.

Nova Scotia Anime and Manga Organization (NSAMO)
190 Chain Lake Drive
Bayers Lake Business Park
Halifax, NS B3S 1C5
Canada
Web site: http://www.nsamo.com
The NSAMO was founded by a group of anime fans in Halifax, Nova Scotia who meet to discuss, watch, swap, and learn about manga. The also have a Web presence and list helpful links for those interested in anime and manga both as artists and consumers.

Society for the Promotion of Japanese Animation
1733 Douglass Road, Suite F

Anaheim, CA 92806
(714) 937-2994
Web site: http://www.spja.org
The Society for the Promotion of Japanese Animation is a
   nonprofit organization dedicated to popularizing the
   unique and deep culture that surrounds Japanese animation by servicing the needs of fans, artists, and the
   industry. They hold an annual conference called the
   Anime Expo which is the largest convention devoted to
   manga and anime.

WEB SITES

Due to the changing nature of Internet links, Rosen
Publishing has developed an online list of Web sites related
to the subject of this book. This site is updated regularly.
Please use this link to access the list:

http://www.rosenlinks.com/mm/boy

FOR FURTHER READING

Flores, Irene. *Shojo Fashion Manga Art School: How to Draw
    Cool Looks and Characters*. New York, NY: Impact, 2009.
Galea, Mario. *Discover Manga Drawing: 30 Easy Lessons for
    Drawing Guys and Girls*. New York, NY: Impact, 2006.
Hart, Christopher. *Manga for the Beginner: Everything You
    Need to Start Drawing Right Away!* New York, NY:
    Watson-Guptill, 2008.
Hart, Christopher. *Manga for the Beginner Shoujo: Everything
    You Need to Start Drawing the Most Popular Style of
    Japanese Comics*. New York, NY: Watson-Guptill, 2010.
Layman, John. *The Complete Idiot's Guide to Drawing Manga*.
    2nd Edition. Royersford, PA: Alpha, 2008.
Myo, Tamimi. *How to Draw Manga: Drawing Bishonen*. Tokyo,
    Japan: Graphic-sha Publishing, 2009.
Okabayashi, Kensuke. *Manga for Dummies*. New York, NY:
    John Wylie & Sons, 2007.
Takarai, Saori. *Manga Moods*. Kawaguchi-shi, Japan: Japanime
    Co., 2006.

INDEX

ABOUT THE AUTHORS

Anna Southgate is an experienced writer and editor who has worked extensively for publishers of adult illustrated reference books. Her recent work has included art instruction books and providing the text for a series of six manga titles.

Keith Sparrow has read and collected comics since he was a child. He has created hundreds of storyboards, including one for the animation movie *Space Jam*, and illustrated several children's educational books for the UK's Channel 4 and the BBC. He became a fan of manga and anime after reading *Akira*.